A W[...]
Cricket Hill

VALERIE KERSLAKE

Laura Pilgrim

With best wishes —
Valerie Kerslake
5 April 1997

ISBN 0 9516061 1 5
© Valerie Kerslake 1996

ACKNOWLEDGMENTS

I should like to thank all those who have helped in the writing of this little book. From members of The Yateley Society I have had help of all sorts, from providing me with old photographs to actually walking the Walk. Michael Holroyd in particular has given me advice, ideas, hard historical facts and sources, and has also been kind enough to read the manuscript. I am most grateful to them all.

Many other people who live or used to live in Yateley have most willingly passed on their memories and local knowledge. It has all been of value and I very much appreciate their help.

Lastly, I thank my husband, David, for his constant encouragement and patience, and for endless computer manoeuvres on my behalf.

Yateley Baptist Church kindly gave me permission to reproduce the sketch of Zoar Chapel from their 150th anniversary booklet. The other illustrations are my own. The drawing of the cottage hospital was taken from an old postcard, and the two of old cottages - Thatch Cottage and the pair of brick cottages which are now part of Casa dei Cesari - are after watercolours by Mrs Georgina Stilwell painted in the 1870s.

A WALK ON CRICKET HILL

Old Cottage, now part of Casa dei Cesari

CRICKET HILL is only three-quarters of a mile from the old centre of Yateley but has something of the character of a small separate village, with a row of cottages bordering Cricket Hill Lane and others grouped along the edge of Yateley Common as if round a village green.

The road on which the small community grew up is old; it is shown as the route between Farnborough and Yateley on a road map of 1675[33], and travellers on foot or horseback must have welcomed the sight of these outposts of Yateley as they came down the rough road across the heath. Several of the cottages have been here for two or three hundred years, although additions and alterations make them difficult to identify. More date from the 19th century and some are quite new. Many of the houses were built on the sites of previous ones, and they too may have replaced still earlier dwellings, the first of which were probably one-room shacks of mud, wood and thatch. It was a place where a poor man might take a piece of the vast "waste", as the heath was called, build some sort of a house for himself or his son, and coax a few crops from the thin acid soil, perhaps to supplement another meagre livelihood. Squatters were always part of this community on the outskirts of Yateley; the well-to-do farmers and craftsmen and the big land-owners lived down in the village, around the Green or along the Reading Road where the land was richer and more fertile.

In 1988 Cricket Hill was designated a Conservation Area by Hart District Council in recognition of its rural, village-like quality, the large number of old cottages and the varied landscape which includes the Royal Oak Valley on the western edge and parts of Yateley Common to the east and south. This walk will be almost entirely within the Conservation Area and begins and ends outside The Cricketers pub.

THE CRICKETERS

Here, as elsewhere, Yateley Common was almost treeless until the mid-twentieth century, the gorse and scrub kept short by grazing animals. The landlord's chickens scratched around in front of the pub and goats were tethered; anyone nearby dashed to release them when there was heath fire. The open grassland and heather was criss-crossed with well-trodden paths taking the shortest route from point to point, almost from house to house. When most people walked or bicycled everywhere they knew all their neighbours and there was a good deal of dropping in on each other.

The Cricketers, which was extended and modernised in 1976, has been in this building since 1928. Before then it was at the white cottage on the right, now a private house called The Old Cricketers. It is one of Cricket Hill's old cottages but has been a good deal altered since its pub days. Earlier generations who walked from Cove to their parish church at Yateley would pause there for refreshment before the final stretch down to the village.

It is not clear when cricket was first played here, though some claim it was nearly as long ago as at Hambledon whose famous cricket club dates from 1750. The name Cricket Hill was used in the 1841 census but no one even knows whether it derives from the game or the insect. There seem to be no records of matches here, and serious cricketers would have joined the Yateley Cricket Club which was founded in 1881 (though a home match against Waltham St Lawrence was reported in the new parish magazine of 1878). There was also the Yateley Junior Cricket Club who played the Eversley Junior Cricket Club in 1866[16]. The game must have been well-established on Cricket Hill by 1881 when The Cricketers Inn is mentioned in the census.

For the twentieth century there are plenty of memories of cricket in front of the pub in the 1920s and early '30s; bicycling over from Blackwater to watch made a favourite Sunday outing for at least one young lad. Teas would be served outside the old Cricketers, boys could earn a penny for finding a lost ball, and home-made ginger pop was sold at the pub for threepence. Especially popular was the Friday evening "old men's match" for the over-seventies.

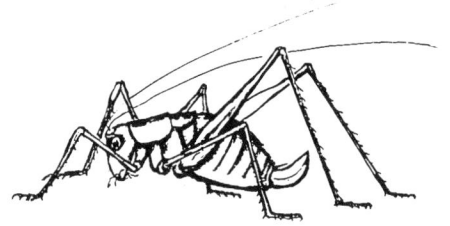

Cricket

SECOND WORLD WAR

The war (1939-45) changed everything. On the east side of Cricket Hill Lane the common was used for tank training, where military exercises had been practised since the 19th century. On the west an airfield was constructed where the fighter/bomber station called Royal Air Force Hartford Bridge was officially opened in November 1942 - though it had been in use since the previous August in spite of no electricity. (After the war it was re-named Blackbushe Airport, but it was not de-requisitioned until 1960.) Before the runways were completed, a glider section from Farnborough established itself here to get away from the planes flying in and out of Farnborough. The glider crews moved into the newly built Nissen huts and pinched half the contents before the other personnel arrived[11]. Free French, Polish and Dutch squadrons joined the RAF, and later the Royal Canadian Air Force. The first arrivals were billetted at Yateley Manor and Eleven Acres in Monteagle Lane (now demolished), but soon huts to accommodate them had been built on almost every piece of open ground, right into the centre of Yateley. Between The Cricketers and Cricket Hill Lane dozens of Nissen huts were erected as quarters for some of the 3000 officers and airmen stationed here by 1943[11].

After the war squatters - chiefly from Yateley and the surrounding villages - moved into the huts which were quickly bought by Hartley Wintney Rural District Council who charged nine shillings and threepence a week rent. The Nissen huts were divided into two by a brick wall, and a cooking range and cold tap were installed at each end. Each family had its own lavatory just outside, and many of them planted colourful gardens around their huts. When the council houses at Manor Park were built about three years after the war, the Nissen hut occupants were moved into them and the huts pulled down. Now the only trace is the odd chunk of half-buried concrete.

Follow the track that leads past The Old Cricketers. The two bungalows beyond it back on to the Royal Oak Valley in which a footpath accompanies a little stream winding through woodland down to the Reading Road.

CHESTNUT COTTAGE AND LEA COTTAGE

A modern house called Moonrakers replaces a pair of "two-up and two-down" cottages - 4 and 3 Chestnut Cottages. Numbers 2 and 1 have been made into one house and recently extended on the right. The left-hand half, which used to be Number 2, was the home of Bill Liddiard throughout his life, and even when he was an old man little had been changed since his birth in 1903, though eventually electricity was installed, and mains water in the form of one cold tap replaced the shared well. He turned down main drainage, however, when it arrived in 1961. The dark and draughty kitchen had racks and large iron rings in the wall for curing joints of bacon, for "everyone kept a pig". A damp patch high in one corner was from the salt in the bacon and would never dry out. Though he eventually had a gas stove, the old kitchen range was still there, with a baker's oven behind it.

Bill started school at three years old (not unusual), walking to the village school on Yateley Green in the care of an older child. As an old man he recalled gleefully how the boys one day put all the head's canes into the stove. The carrier brought another gross from Reading and a boy threw all of them into the pond. Young Bill sometimes failed to touch his cap when he passed "the old Squire" (Mr Stilwell) and then he would be called back with "Boy, do you know who I am?" John Stilwell's son, Geoffrey Holt Stilwell, would walk along in front of the cottages with pockets full of chestnuts, planting alternate red and white ones. Bill thought this pretty silly but others remember with pleasure their blossoming each May. Only one tree survives today.

Behind Chestnut Cottages lay allotment gardens on which cottagers grew fruit and vegetables and perhaps kept bees or chickens. They and the fields below them were eventually sold for development in the twentieth century with large houses in large gardens gradually filling the area from south of the Reading Road up to Cricket Hill. A narrow footpath on the right of Chestnut Cottage leads down to a network of footpaths and private roads giving access to these houses.

Parts of Lea Cottage, on the further side of the footpath, date from 1830, parts from the previous century. The two rooms on the left, however, were added in the 1960s - the different brickwork can be distinguished. Until then the outside wall on that side had an old brick bread oven bulging out of it, while in the front room on the right there used to be rows of iron hooks and rings for hanging the bacon. The conical tower is for the water tank and was added by the Stilwells when they owned the house after one of them had seen such towers in Germany.

Lea Cottage was for twenty-five years the home of Colonel John Lathbury who devoted much of this time to work for the Yateley and Hawley branch of the Royal British Legion. As chairman, he took on innumerable jobs including organising the poppy appeal, and his regular visits to older or housebound members were often the highlight of the week for them. After his death in 1985 a plaque in his memory was placed on the common opposite.

"The Colonels' Acre" was the name given to this part of Cricket Hill just after the Second World War - so many army families lived here. Yateley was discovered to be a desirable village soon after the Royal Military College moved to Sandhurst in 1812. The Staff College opened in 1862 and Aldershot Camp was not far away, so there was always a steady flow of officers wanting a nice house in an accessible and pleasant village. Only in the 1960s when Yateley was turning into a town had they begun to leave, with developers often buying their houses.

LINGFIELD SCHOOL AND CRICKET HILL COTTAGE

On the corner is Cricket Hill Cottage, formerly Lingfield and for a while known as St George's Cottage. It was built about 1880 with the brick and tile-hung walls popular at that time, and replaced a pair of cottages that were burnt down shortly before. Lingfield School for Young Ladies was opened here about 1890 by Mrs Wilding and flourished for some years until it outgrew its accommodation and moved to Camberley. The late Margaret Christison, daughter of John Mills of Holly Hill (now demolished) in Potley Hill Road, joined the school in 1899, and remembered her headmistress with affection and admiration:

"A widow...with two daughters to bring up, she came to Yateley as governess to the Misses Stilwell. She lived in the house on... the side of the Hilfield barnyard... Here she discovered an opening for taking charge of girls whose parents were abroad. Moving to Lingfield she gathered more children, more than the house would hold. So she took the cottage on the other side of the road...and that proving too small left it for the double-fronted cottage next up the hill which had formerly had a shop window where the girls could buy sweets (2 oz a penny!) and cheap exercise books and pencils - slate and lead! By now there was an English governess who was in charge at the cottage, and a French teacher... Day girls were added, we were about 20 in all. Young Miss Wilding taught 4 days a week, going to Reading for art classes twice weekly... The younger sister, Miss Winnie, taught the youngest class and "Calisthenics", Swedish exercises, and fancy displays - rod drill, scarf exercises and other refinements. Drill was taken by the current Drill Sergeant, Sergt. Hilton of the Volunteers, and then by Sergt. Sillence of the T.A. Discipline was good, rules were not many but they were very definite. Much attention was paid to posture and Mrs Wilding believed in Elegance, which she regretted was being neglected. Four days a week we had "Bible Class" with her to start the morning. We read a portion of Scripture verse by verse round the table. This was then applied to the daily life of School - tidiness, etc. I believe some of the most useful lessons were learnt during General Knowledge. At any spare moment we were asked, or allowed to ask, questions on any imaginable subject. If our views and that of our teacher disagreed we were allowed to bring evidence for our view.

"The education was sound, suitable pupils being sent into Reading to take Oxford Local, Junior and Senior Exams. We were taught to learn, what more could we ask?"

Elsewhere Margaret Christison says, "There was no bathroom at Lingfield. The sanitation - if it could be so called - at the house was a bucket earth closet opening out of the hall, and at the cottages just outside pits!" (It should be remembered that although this was a newly-built and quite substantial house, all water used indoors had to be pumped up from a well. Main water and drainage did not come for another sixty years.)

She stayed at Lingfield until she was eighteen and never regretted being educated at "that sometimes laughed at institution, a School for Young Ladies". She went on to a career in medicine[2].

One famous old *boy* can be claimed by Lingfield, the painter Paul Nash, who as a small child used to come to Yateley to stay with his aunt, Mrs Chapman. She thought it high time he went to school and took him to meet Mrs Wilding. In his autobiography he does not remember learning much at the school but greatly enjoyed the walk from Harpton House in Vicarage Road across the fields and over the little stream to Cricket Hill[13].

In the 20th century Cricket Hill Cottage was bought by Colonel F. D. M. Brown, VC, and his son, Major General Llewellyn Brown, continued to live here until his death in 1983. General Brown was Director General of the Ordnance Survey from 1949 to 1953. He was a keen advocate of air survey, even learning to fly, and did not let the loss of his right arm while on survey work in the 1920s in any way hinder his career[26]. A wooden lychgate was built at the Pipson Lane entrance to the churchyard in 1938 as a memorial to his father and other relations, but repeated vandalism and arson in the 1990s forced the church to consider its demolition.

Another distinguished member of this family was his only sister, Jessie Brown, MBE, who was a pioneer in the field of orthopaedic after-care nursing, and devoted her life to the care of others. She has been described too as being "outstandingly pretty, with tremendous vitality and a strong sense of fun, and also a talented artist"[3]. In Yateley she is best known for founding Yateley Textiles. Here in a garden shed she and a friend who had suffered from polio tried out hand block printing of textiles, a technique she had seen while nursing in India and had thought might be a rewarding occupation for the disabled. It worked well enough for her to have a small workshop for eight disabled girls set up in Moulsham Lane in 1937, which flourished and expanded to become today's well-known Yateley Industries[37].

CRICKET HILL LANE

Before leaving Cricket Hill Cottage, notice the sarsen stone propped beside its small front gate. Sarsens are masses of hard sandstone left millions of years ago after the softer deposit containing them had weathered away. They are found in south-east England and there are several in Yateley, including one built into the foundations of St Peter's church by the north porch.

Now go up the hill towards the corner of Handford Lane. It may be pleasanter to be a little further from the traffic and walk inside the bushes along the edge of the common. In summer the grass beside you, which has never been improved with fertiliser or weedkiller, is a meadow of wild flowers - vetches, clovers, cranesbill, knapweed, tansy, ox-eye daisies. It is cut for hay each August when the seeds have fallen.

Although commercial grazing had ceased altogether before the last war, Daphne Kirkpatrick used to graze her three cows and two ponies here for several years after it. She lived opposite at Moorside, and right up to her death in 1995 pursued her determined efforts to guard the rights of commoners in order to preserve the common for future generations. Moorside dates from before 1815 but had considerable additions later in the century.

MAYNARD'S STORES

The white house with black shutters that faces down Handford Lane is called Grasshoppers today, but there are people who still remember it as Maynard's stores - a baker's and general store that stocked "whatever people asked for". Previously it had been a public house called The Prince of Wales, but Mr Maynard had already set up his baker's shop here at the time of the 1891 census where he traded for more than thirty years. Between the wars it had another useful function: a blue sign hung outside saying "You may telephone from here".

VENTILATING BRICKS

Turn back down the hill again. The little smithy set back from the road functioned as a farrier's for some years but nowadays ready-made horseshoes with a gas burner to heat them on are taken to the horse instead. The house next to it was built to replace a pair of ramshackle old cottages demolished in the early 1980s. One was occupied by the Bull family during the last quarter of the 19th century. Young Annie Bull started work as a kitchen maid but inherited from her mother - and her father before that - the job of postwoman, and for many years delivered letters and parcels all over the village every day of the week in her governess cart. She was said to have blown a trumpet when she had something for you, though possibly this depended upon the status of the recipient.

When one of the cottages was being pulled down, the ground floor wall of a kitchen extension at the back was discovered to have been made of very curious bricks - three inches thick but nine inches square with a large semi-circle cut out of two opposite sides, though from both outside and inside of the building it looked an ordinary nine-inch wall. They seem to have been one of the many brick-making inventions which did not really catch on, although they are mentioned in a treatise on brick manufacturing of 1850, where they are called "ventilating bricks", and described as "especially suited to the construction of flued walls for hothouses, gaols, washhouses, and other buildings, which it may be desirable to warm without using open fires"[4]. When laid  as a wall, these bricks would leave a spindle-shaped gap about three inches long between the overlapping bricks, through which air might circulate.

In the case of this cottage, ventilation was not a consideration as the holes had been carefully filled with stones and rubble. However, there were advantages in cost. There had been Brick Taxes between 1784 and 1850, but one of these bricks, which contained the same amount of clay as one common brick though filling the space of two, was liable for the duty on only a single common brick[4]. In addition, a cartload of ventilating bricks was only half the weight.

Another piece of simple technology was found about 1960 when the meadows in the valley behind were being drained. Earlier land drains were still in place, U-shaped with no top but with a foot of heather piled above them. U-shaped pipes would have been cheap to buy as they could be made by simply hanging a square of clay over a pole, while heather used to be abundant and is supposed never to rot.

THE NEST AND THATCH COTTAGE

Going down the hill, after Moorside you will see the tiled roof of a tiny cottage called The Nest. This is a Grade II listed building dating from about 1750, and it is where the first Baptists in Yateley met before they built their chapel opposite in 1827. The roof, half-hipped at one end, was probably thatched to begin with; its steep pitch would have encouraged the rain to run off. At the back is a catslide, which is a long roof running almost down to the ground - an economical way of roofing an extra room behind a one-room-deep house. The extra room was usually a kitchen, with in this case a large larder beside it, and a big open fireplace and bread oven which were boarded up and undiscovered for many years. It is a timber framed building with chequered Flemish bond brickwork on the front wall where red stretchers alternate with blue-grey headers - rather fashionable in the 18th and early 19th century and probably added to the original cottage. The recently filled-in porch has brickwork to match. The chimney stack on the left has an oddly incongruous squared white chimney pot, a popular style in Georgian and Regency days[1]. Similar pots can be seen more appropriately on Yateley Lodge at the bottom of the hill, and also on Chaddisbrook House beside the church.

All the cottages in this row have been enlarged in one way or another; in the case of The Nest, it has been linked by a glazed passage to the one next door which appears to be an attractive jumble of old brick walls, beams and tiled roofs but was actually built quite recently with old materials.

Thatch Cottage, half hidden behind its holly hedge, and seemingly sliding down the hillside like its neighbours, is also timber-framed and Grade II listed. It may date from the 18th century, for although the date 1801 is scratched on the wall above the porch (hidden by the thatch) the brick façade could have been added to an earlier structure. Inside there are numerous unstained oak timbers. From the front, Thatch Cottage is typical of the small houses one might have found in Yateley over a period of several centuries, though this one would have been more solidly built than many or it would not have survived.

A water-colour by Mrs Georgina Stilwell (or possibly one of her daughters) shows the cottage in the 1870s almost entirely swathed in red and green creepers. There is a very trim barn a few yards to the right of the cottage, but the one-storey extension on that side does not appear. Today's house has a larger extension being constructed by the present owners at the back on the left. Thatch, old bricks and beams have been used so skilfully that it is hard to distinguish old from new, inside or out.

Further down is Wayside, which Mrs Wilding took for some of her pupils and where they had been able to buy sweets and pencils. Toys too, for one old man remembered with nostalgia for seventy years a sailing yacht in the window to which he had taken a great fancy[9]. It is said that the house was built as a pub though that plan fell through. It is given distinction by the rather grand carved swag of fruit and flowers in the centre of a stone string course.

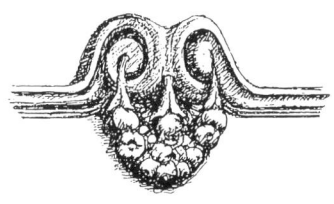

In 1859 White's Directory[31] mentions Sarah Rackley as running a grocer's shop near here. It seems most likely to have been Rose Cottage, the last in the row, in spite of the date 1861 above the porch, and the shop may well have been in the one-storey extension on the left of the house. It was still in business at the census of 1881 when Miss Rackley was 77.

On the opposite side of the road a magnificent tree house in an oak just below Cricket Hill Cottage used to be a landmark for every traveller down Cricket Hill Lane. It was built before the last war by Colonel Buck who lived at Oakhurst (then a bungalow) with the help of a team of his son's friends from Wellington College. All the local children used to play in it, and Wellington boys would be invited to tea up the tree where up to fourteen could be squeezed in. The maid would carry out the tea to the lift and it was hauled up to the tree house where Mrs Buck herself would pour. Tree and tree house were lost when the road was widened in 1971.

WELLMORE

A few houses further down is Wellmore, half hidden behind a cypress hedge. It was considerably extended and modernised in 1937 but the right hand end is a half-timbered cottage built perhaps four hundred years ago. In the mid-nineteenth century it was Samuel Paice's baker's shop until bought by John Stilwell who was rapidly acquiring a great deal of local property. In the 1870s and '80s successive governesses to his family lived here - at least one finding it very damp[12]. In north Hampshire the word "moor" meant wet heath, which in this case may refer - if not to the cottage itself - to the marshy land across the road.

Just beyond the cottage was the Stilwell barnyard and immediately past it a footpath led across the fields to St Peter's Church. The footpath, no doubt old then, is still there though part of it is now an unmade road which starts as Beaver Lane and then becomes Old Welmore. But there are no fields today.

STONEYCROFT AND BRONZE AGE URNS

You are now out of the traffic in a comparatively quiet backwater created by the 1971 road improvements to Cricket Hill Lane[36]. (Only thirty years earlier it had been a real lane - narrow, winding, gravelled and steep enough to defeat the coalman's horse in wet weather when the cart was heavily loaded.) Stoneycroft Cottage up the bank beside you is an old cottage with a curious modern history. Until the 1980s it was one of a pair, but the owner of the right hand side wished to detach his part and eventually succeeded in doing so, re-building it to look not dissimilar but a few feet to the right.

Tree House

When you reach the end of the lay-by you will be able to see a reedy marsh on the other side of the road. It is all that remains of the small lake in the grounds of the Stilwells' house, Hilfield, and was the centre of all sorts of jollifications. Their eldest daughter, Norah, wrote years later of the fun the family and their friends had on The Pond in the 1870s and '80s: "In summer there were the boats, punt and bathing. In winter skating, hockey matches on the ice for several winters... We had a yearly match against Wellington College... Then there were parties, figure skating... illuminations at night, mulled claret, hot coffee, cakes and muffins etc, etc. All the Hilfield workmen swept the ice daily for us so it was kept in very good order"[19].

Turn left now into Quarry Lane. The garden beyond the hedge on the right is on the site of a gravel pit where fragments of Late Bronze Age pottery (dating perhaps from 700 to 600 BC) were discovered in

1926[17]. They range from pieces of a large urn, fifteen inches in diameter and richly decorated with zig-zags of impressed cord-pattern decoration, to a small food vessel less than four inches high[15].

Bronze Age remains have been found elsewhere in Yateley - close by at Rounds Close where there was a cinerary urn containing the burnt bones of a child, and, most notably, at Moor Place in Moulsham Lane where gravel digging in the 1920s uncovered an occupation site with hearth, cooking places, a bronze cup, pottery and loom weights. These and other sites indicate extensive prehistoric settlements along the Blackwater Valley, concentrated particularly around Yateley and Farnham[23].

A short way up the lane is Quarry House, one of several large, handsome houses in the Tudor style erected in this area in the 1920s by the Yateley builder, B.A.Fullbrook. Old barns provided the half-timbering and the roof tiles. The sunken garden in front of the house was previously a gravel pit, giving its name to both house and lane. Quarry House and its neighbour beyond are bounded by a delightfully fantastic wall of burnt bricks of various shades laid on their sides. **Continue along this unmade road, turning left when you reach the junction with Old Welmore and then left into Beaver Lane.** The larger houses in this area, which is loosely known as Old Welmore, date mainly from between the wars, but after the Second World War some were demolished, or their extensive gardens divided up for smaller houses more in keeping with a world from which domestic servants had almost vanished.

HILFIELD AND STEVENS HILL

When you get back to Cricket Hill Lane, cross over and go up Stevens Hill. The residential estate on the left was built in the 1970s on Hilfield, the former property of the Stilwell family whose name has cropped up on almost every page of this walk. John Pakenham Stilwell, JP, (1832-1921) was a wealthy

London banker who came to Yateley after his wife, Georgina Stevens, inherited Hilfield from her parents in 1871. They soon became leading figures in the community, generous with both time and money and in supporting village activities from the cricket club to the Volunteers. He and his wife donated many of the furnishings for the church after its restoration in 1878. He sang in the choir and was church-warden for years as well as Chairman of the Parish Council. When in 1900 Conservators of Yateley Common had been appointed under the Ecclesiastical Commissioners, John Stilwell became their secretary, and, as his daughter recorded with pride, he with fellow members successfully resisted a proposal to enclose Yateley Common[18].

The early Victorian mansion that had been built on to an older and more modest house was destroyed by fire in 1900 and replaced by one still larger, later to be known as Yateley Place. This was demolished for development in 1973, catching fire during the process - a strange echo of the earlier conflagration. Little remains but the great cedar planted in front of the old house; it can be seen from Cricket Hill Lane. The Hilfield estate was sold when the Stilwell family fortune was ravaged by two lots of death duties in quick succession after John's son, Geoffrey Holt Stilwell, was knocked off his bicycle in Blackwater in 1927. Most of John Stilwell's children, however, continued to live in various cottages around the village, three of his daughters moving up the hill to Moorside. The small house up amongst the trees on the corner of the road to the cemetery was built by a grandson after the second world war. It too is called Stevens Hill, after the family who once owned the land on both sides of the road. Today there are no Stilwells left in Yateley.

This lane once ran straight from Cricket Hill Lane to the corner of Cobbetts Lane and Rounds Close, but an earlier occupant of Hilfield - it had long been a rich man's estate - did what many landowners used to do and in 1821 applied for a diversion order to move the road further from the front of his house[29]. The result is an elbow-like bend half way along.

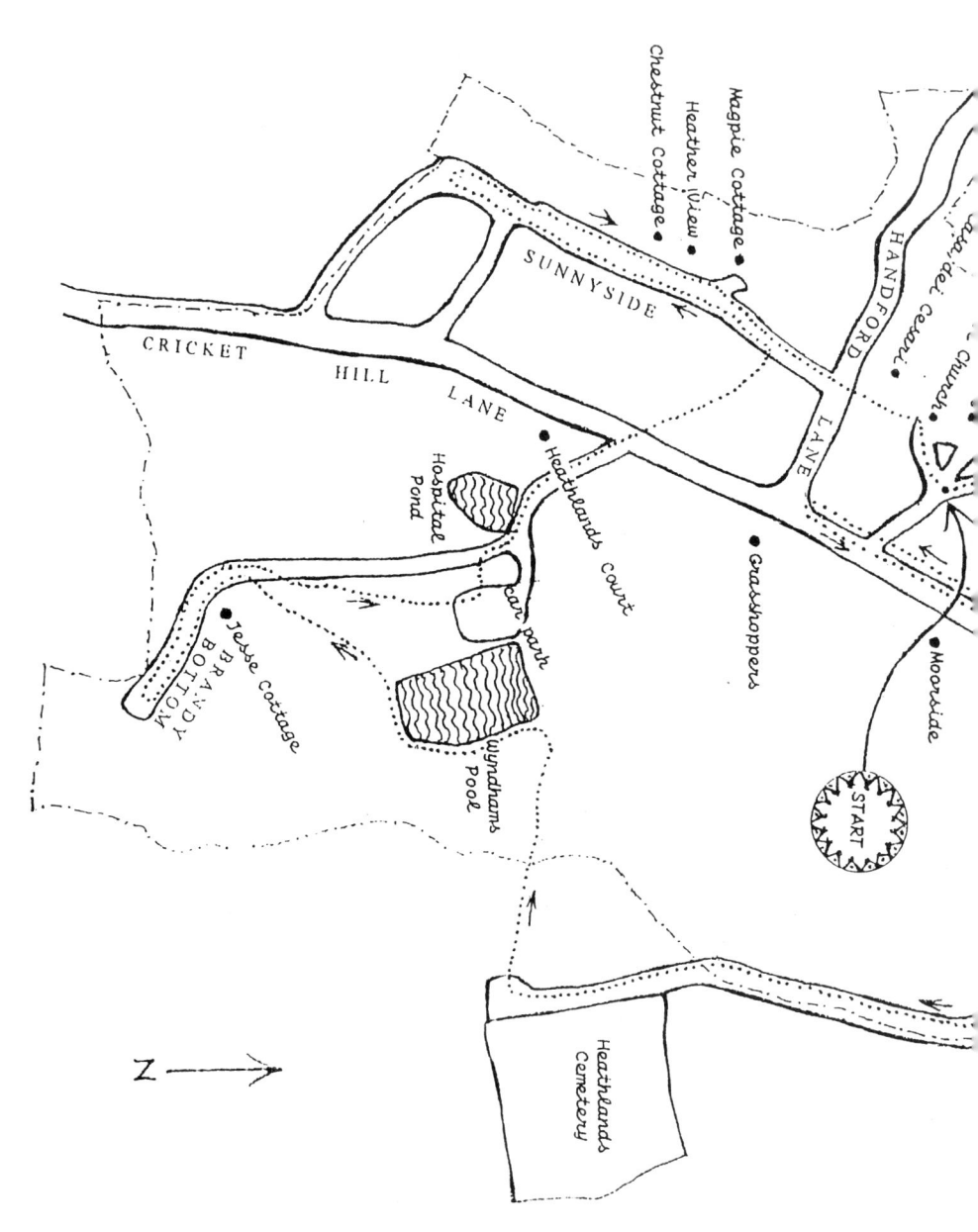

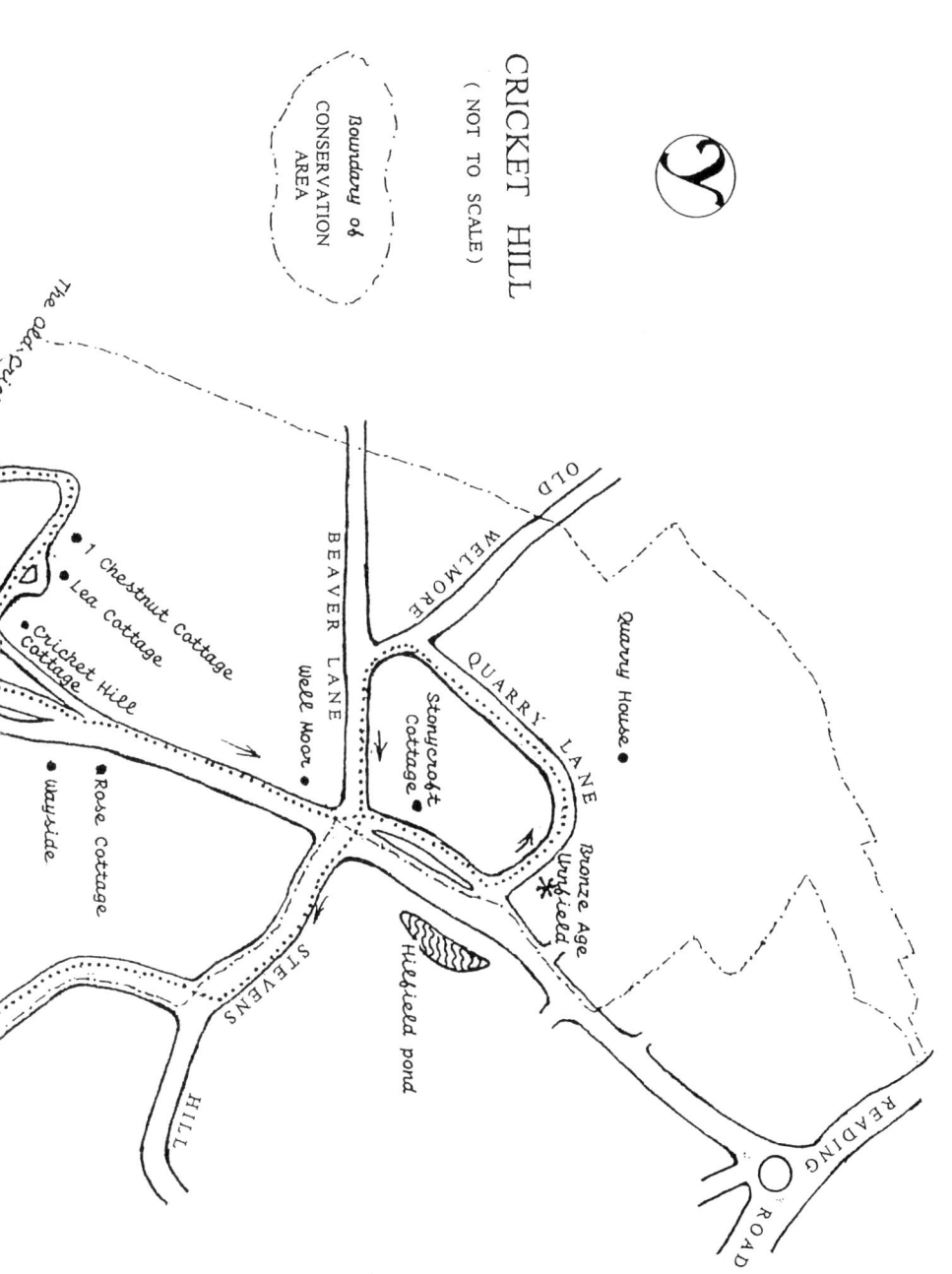

Do not walk as far as that, but turn right along the road to the cemetery and the common. In a moment you pass Thriftswood, a pretty house set in woodland and lawns, which was built in 1929 for Geoffrey Stilwell's widow. The architect was A.C.Martin, a pupil of Lutyens. Notice the Dutch gable echoing the arched doorway below, and the diaper pattern in red and blue brickwork on the façade. It must have been a picturesque setting for the Boxing Day meet of the RMA Sandhurst Hunt which Mrs Stilwell welcomed to her house both before and after the last war.

After Thriftswood's small paddock, Yateley Common begins, an uncharacteristic section with birches and old oaks growing out of a switchback of hummocks and hollows created by gravel digging, where not so many years ago there were badger setts amongst the tree roots. Gravel was not always free although commoners might take it for their personal use. When the Turnpike road (A30) between Blackwater Bridge and Hartford Bridge was to be repaired in 1819, the Vestry (who ran parish affairs before parish councils were formed in 1894) were responsible for having the work carried out, and they resolved that the price for digging gravel for the project should be sixpence per (cart)load[35]. A hundred years later, a Yateley builder recalled, it cost one shilling a load.

HILL FARM

Beyond the fringe of trees on the left (with bluebells under them in May) are the green fields of Hill Farm, one of the last two farms in a village which was once all farms, and where cultivated fields ran northwards from here down to the River Blackwater. In the nineteenth century the farms began to be amalgamated, becoming larger but fewer, and were later gradually sold off piecemeal[20]. There were still smallholders in the 1920s with comparatively little land who grazed large numbers of cattle and sheep on the common but this had ceased by the start of the Second World War in 1939. By the 1960s most of the remaining fields were being turned into housing estates, schools and playing fields.

There is a particular historical interest about Hill Farm and some of the land around it, in that the field boundaries have been more or less unchanged since medieval times. Their names and areas correspond with descriptions in the 1567 Crondall Customary which listed all the lands and copyholders (tenants) of the Lord of the Manor. The old field names persisted into the nineteenth century and can then be related to a pre-1817 estate map[32] and the 1844 Tithe Map[7].

HEATHLANDS CEMETERY AND YATELEY COMMON

You will now be passing Heathlands Cemetery, which was opened in 1957 on heathland provided by Yateley Parish Council when the churchyard was almost full, the commoners agreeing to give up their rights for the area required.

At that time Yateley Parish Council owned a large part of Yateley Common which had been bought in 1951 from the Church Commissioners (successors to the Ecclesiastical Commissioners). It proved to be expensive to manage and there were problems with gypsies[9], but their real troubles began in 1961 when Air-Vice Marshall Donald Bennett bought the western end of the common from Lord Calthorpe on which lay most of the structures of the old airfield. Only the eastern ends of the runways and half a building were on Parish Council land. Air-Vice Marshall Bennett intended to open a commercial airport, but to do this effectively wanted a strip of the Parish Council's land, and they were not willing to sell, wishing to keep the whole common as public open space. The Air-Vice Marshall was persistent and eventually the Parish Council were advised to transfer their part of the common to Hampshire County Council who would be better able to withstand the pressure. The transfer went through in 1964[27], with the Parish Council retaining only Yateley, Moulsham, Darby and Frogmore Greens[9]. Four years later the Parish Council realised that the piece of common in front of The Cricketers had been transferred to Hampshire - probably in error. They thought it could have been developed as a children's playground but it has remained the property of Hampshire[36]. Nowadays Yateley Common is a Country Park and is in the care of full-time rangers. It has been designated a Site of Special Scientific Interest and a Special Protection Area (a European Union designation for rare birds), and is also part of the Forest of Eversley Heritage Area.

When you reach the main gates of the cemetery, take the footpath opposite that leads through scrub and heather to Wyndhams Pool. In winter it may look sombre but under the heather there is bright green moss and perhaps delicate blue-green lichens with scarlet spore capsules, while there are few days when you cannot find a few yellow flowers on the gorse. The large common gorse is most brilliant from April to June when it fills the air with the scent of coconut; dwarf gorse flowers from July into the autumn. July and August are also when the heather is at its finest; it is mainly ling, with patches of magenta bell heather, and in damp places there is cross-leaved heath which has whorls of four bluish-grey leaves up the stem and rather large pale pink flowers. Notice too the Wavy Hair-grass which grows freely on poor, acid soils. It has short, bristle-like leaves and stems that are sometimes tinged with red. The waviness lies in the hair-like branches leading to pairs of shining, pinkish flower spikelets.

In warm weather you may come across a lizard, grass snake or adder basking in the sun - all will vanish in a flash if they sense your footsteps or see your shadow. Occasionally in winter one finds a fragile silvery snakeskin, usually amongst the larger heather bushes where the snake has rubbed off its old skin against the woody stalks.

Adder

Heathland butterflies are numerous. The little Silver-studded Blue is one of the prettiest and flocks of them can sometimes be found hovering over clumps of heather. Less easy to see is the Grayling which rests on the ground with only its blotchy, greyish-brown hind wings visible. It further disguises itself by tilting towards the sun to minimise its shadow.

Dartford Warbler

You will pass tree stumps; felling is carried out regularly by the rangers, often with the help of volunteers. The aim is to restore the heath, which means not just heather but the many plants, insects, reptiles, birds and mammals, from harvest mouse to roe deer, that flourish on this poor sandy heathland soil. Many species cannot survive elsewhere. Two hundred years ago lowland heath like this covered huge swathes of Surrey, Hampshire and Dorset but it is now so reduced that it is regarded as an internationally rare habitat. Where it has been lost to roads and development it is too late to recover, but trees that have sprung up in the past half century can be removed and the heathland plants encouraged to spread across the ground again. Some trees are being left to enhance the landscape, and also gorse bushes to attract heathland birds such as the stonechat and rare Dartford warbler.

Heathland was formed artificially several thousand years ago by our distant ancestors (perhaps the Bronze Age chaps who made the urns?) clearing parts of the forest to grow crops and graze their animals, but the poor soil was soon exhausted and heathland plants moved in. The heath however still provided them with grazing and also gravel, turf, furze and wood for fuel and houses. Such resources continued to be valued right up to a hundred years ago, with villagers seeing the heath as an essential part of their economy, and keeping it in good heart by grazing and gathering fuel and turf[21], and controlled burning-off in February to encourage fresh growth of grass and heather.

WYNDHAMS POOL

Following the path downhill you will see Wyndhams Pool gleaming between the trees. This beautiful lake is thought to have been made by Thomas Wyndham (1695-1763), a rich and well-connected man who came to live at Hall Place (now Yateley Manor) after marrying a Yateley heiress[5]. The lake is formed by a barrier beneath the concrete causeway along the northern end, which dams the little stream which is known as the Pottle when it gets further down the hill. But turn left here along the side of the pool (it may be muddy further on; if in doubt go along the causeway instead); and see the ducks, water-lilies and trees reflected in the water. Imagine now how it looked sixty years ago when it was Yateley's bathing pond. There were no trees, no lilies, but seats all around on the bare sloping banks. Countless Yateley people learnt to swim here and remember the clear water and sandy bottom, and the fun they all had. In summer and on holidays it was "like Brighton", with paddling and picnics and games on the banks, and ice cream for sale. Water-wings could be improvised from half-gallon oil cans retrieved from rubbish dumps. There was skating and hockey on the ice in winter, but fishing was restricted to the pool below the old cottage hospital which you will pass later. Wyndhams is where one fishes nowadays, but bathing is forbidden, even for dogs.

This pool which looks so permanent has had a rather sporadic existence. It does not appear on the 1871 Ordnance Survey map except as an area of marsh, although the pool and the Hospital Pond as well are shown on the first one-inch OS map which was published in 1816, for which this area was surveyed in 1806[6]. It is back again on the 1896 OS map, so presumably there had been a period when it became totally silted up and overgrown as often happens when ponds are neglected.

During the Second World War Wyndhams was drained, as were other lakes, to prevent enemy aircraft navigating by them. A sheet of water in the moonlight is conspicuous from the air. It was refilled soon after the war but all the water was washed out again in a thunderstorm a little later. It was not until the early 1950s that another, successful, attempt was made by the village policeman, PC Eric Short, who enlisted the help of local youngsters to help build a new dam (later concreted over by the council) and to clear a mass of young birches now growing all over the floor of the pool. The diving board whose remains stick starkly out of the water was put up by PC Short too, and again for a few years it was a popular bathing pool until Hampshire County Council put up a notice saying "No bathing, no boating". By then birches and pines were springing up all around. The new wooded face of the common was emerging.

At the end of the path turn right.
The fence around the corner is to prevent exuberant dogs from dashing into this marshy patch where dragonflies are encouraged to breed. On the left amongst damp sphagnum moss there may be sundews - a tiny carnivorous plant whose leaves are covered with sticky red hairs that capture small insects. The plant absorbs and digests them to supplement the meagre diet it receives from the poor soil. As you go along it will become more and more swampy on your left; somewhere amongst the tangle of willow, reedmace, rushes and waterweeds is the spring whose water fills Wyndhams Pool and runs on down to the River Blackwater. Dragonflies, and damselflies, their slender relations, flourish; 23 species were recorded here in the early 1980s, out of the 37 species breeding in Great Britain.

Sundew

The muddy path you are on was constructed by the RAF in the 1940s, and the big concrete discs on each side were bases for landing lights to guide planes on to the landing strip at Blackbushe.

BRANDY BOTTOM

Bear left up the slope at the end of the path until you reach the unmade road that leads to the row of houses known as Brandy Bottom. Jesse Cottage at this end was one of the first two to be built; they are very obvious examples of encroachment in the early nineteenth century. It was cases like this that caused the Vestry to appoint two common keepers in 1821 and to perambulate the parish boundaries. Expenses for this procedure were to be borne by those having rights of common for turf and pasturage[35]. These first cottages appear on the Tithe Map of 1844 on adjoining plots of a little over half an acre each. The 1871 Ordnance Survey map shows a second house on each plot, while on the 1896 OS map there are nine houses in the row and an extra one has gained a piece of land opposite the end. A hundred years later the houses are so much larger that there is little space between them although there are now only eight. The area originally enclosed has expanded over the years - people have always been greedy about land and will push out their fences or replant their hedges to gain a few feet here or there. Pigsties and even clothes posts have been used to claim possession; if they can get away with it for twelve years they may well have won it[35].

The first men who lived here were labourers; indeed agricultural labourer was the commonest occupation in the country around the middle of the 19th century. By the 1870s there are references[12] to the Brandy Bottom laundresses - a desperately hard job before the days of electricity and when all water had to be drawn and carried from a well, but it brought in a little extra money. There seem to have been laundresses here for several decades, with the laundry run by Mrs Davis who employed a number of local women remaining in business until the late 1920s. Washing lines were strung along the grass opposite the cottages.

Little Acre, half way along, retains a Victorian charm with its verandah and tile-hung walls. Although it was built in 1864, the title deeds indicate that these features were probably added by the builder Henry Bunch who bought half the house in 1886 for £20, to sell three years later for £250. James Coles, a labourer with a large family who was the first occupant of the house, failed to make anything like Mr Bunch's handsome profit, selling the second half in 1889 for £50.

Next door at Jesse Cottage lived William Coles, probably James's brother or cousin. He had seven sons, the middle one named Jesse, and perhaps it was he who inherited the cottage and gave it his name.

Small houses seldom had names before the late 19th century but were referred to by the name of the occupant. Most of the original Jesse Cottage has vanished inside its extensions, but as you turn back along the track you can see part of the chequered brick wall on the western side that does belong to the old cottage. The windows have been replaced.

If you should come across an extra large snail shell, creamy with pale brown markings, amongst the brambles and long grass of Brandy Bottom, it is probably from a small colony of Roman or "edible" snails. They are widespread on the continent and can also sometimes be found in south-east England where the Romans are said to have introduced them.

The name Brandy Bottom has never been satisfactorily explained in spite of some ingenious and picturesque ideas. Some say it was just a children's nickname. Its first appearance seems to have been on a census form in 1871, but it has never been shown on an OS map. The census enumerator of 1851 called it Cricket Bottom.

THE HOSPITAL POND AND THE SCHOOL

Walk along the grass above the road, with Wyndhams Pool below you on the right. The car park you soon come to won a design award when it was constructed in the early 1980s though alterations were soon necessary to stop it being used as a race track. **Take the little path or the drive down from it and cross the track from Brandy Bottom;** you will shortly be beside the Hospital Pond, known earlier as School Pond or Boseley's pond. Today this is a nature reserve where ducks and moorhens breed. In the past it was the fishing pond, and elderly fishermen still remember the smell of chloroform that used to drift across from the hospital. It had more practical uses as well: horses had to be watered, and in dry weather carts needed to be hauled through water to prevent the wooden wheels shrinking away from their iron rims - there was a lead-in and a lead-out for the carters. When steam engines came in they too required ponds as they could not go far without being filled up.

Yateley used to have more ponds than today; they could be made by damming any of the little streams that run down from the common. You can see the stream leaving the pond here on the right of the road; the deep hollow is an old gravel pit.

The high brick buildings above the pond are called Heathlands Court and are not the hospital which was pulled down in 1988 by Hart District Council in order to build accommodation for homeless families.

This site was originally chosen for Yateley's first proper school, built in 1834 on common land given by the Lord of the Manor, and made possible by the National Society, a Church of England organisation for promoting primary education. It remained the village school until the new one opened on the Green in 1865 (now the Village Hall), although there is a story that Captain Mason of Yateley Manor built one on part of his land in the centre of the village (now Manor Cottage). That school had a short life and the children went back to Cricket Hill[20] which, though handy for the young Coleses, was a long walk for others. A child was required to pay a penny or two a week until the Elementary Education Act of 1891.

There were also "dame schools", where the children sat round on stools in a small cottage room, paying a few pence a week but seldom learning very much. A legacy by Mary Barker in 1704 seems to have encouraged a crop of these in the 18th and 19th centuries. She left money to be divided between Yateley and two other parishes for the purpose of appointing in each parish "a sober, pious and able Protestant Schoolmaster or Schoolmistress, who shall diligently and carefully teach and instruct such of the poor inhabitants of the .....Parishes as shall be for the purpose named by the Trustees .....to read the Holy Bible in the English tongue, and each Schoolmistress to teach the poor female children to sew and make plain work, and to knit"[20]. In the mid-nineteenth century there were dame schools in Chandlers Lane and at Trythes (now Forge Court) which some parents may have thought to be warmer or preferred to the long walk up to Cricket Hill. Though children, like their parents, were used to walking, they often lacked adequate clothing and footwear for cold or wet weather, and many suffered so dreadfully from chilblains in winter that putting on their hard boots at all must have been impossible[8].

The school was sold in 1865 to Henry Boseley, a market gardener who lived there about thirty years. He had inherited some £2000 in Consols from an ancestor who made a lucky speculation in the Napoleonic wars. When asked one day by the vicar, the Reverend C. D. Stooks, if he had made a will, he said no, but he meant to leave it all to the government because they paid his interest so punctually every quarter. Mr Stooks dissuaded him from doing this and advised leaving it to his relations, but that Boseley would not do on any account. A cottage hospital was suggested but he wished to benefit old men who had seen better days and eventually left it to the Royal Agricultural Benevolent Institution. After his death, however, and before his house and garden were sold, a Mrs Trenchard who lived on the opposite side of Cricket Hill also died, leaving £250 for a cottage hospital, which when topped up with £100 by the Trustees was enough to purchase Boseley's house and found the hospital[20].

THE COTTAGE HOSPITAL

Yateley Cottage Hospital before 1930

With Trustees and some funds already in hand, Yateley was clearly only waiting for premises to join the cottage hospital movement. That had begun in 1859 and within twenty years there were cottage hospitals in villages in every county. Subscriptions large and small were raised from well-wishers to provide a cottage with a nurse and beds (eight at first in Yateley) and put it at the disposal of the local doctor. The hospitals were originally intended for the "respectable poor" and patients were required to pay, even if only sixpence a week. (The humbler poor could apply for help from the Poor Law medical officer[8].)

The hospital was of enormous value to Yateley and the surrounding villages. All the run-of-the-mill operations were carried out by the local doctors. It is said that Mr Harvey, who in the 1920s lived in Yateley but had a Harley Street practice, would perform any operation here apart from brain surgery. The single-storey white building was extended several times, with a second storey and then an adjoining block until it had about twenty beds. A memorial plaque on its walls read:

> The nurses and staff quarters were built
> in memory of the late
> Mrs A. W. MACRAE
> by her daughter
> to commemorate her great interest
> in the hospital and its staff
> 1936

Local people gave it unflagging support; there were bazaars, garden parties, raffles, hospital days and Queen Alexandra's Rose Day, when the collection went to the hospital. Those who lived nearby brought vegetables from their gardens, and half of Yateley would squeeze on to the lawn between hospital and pond for the annual fete.

In due course the hospital was taken over by the National Health Service, but its closure in 1974 after Frimley Park Hospital had opened was seen as the saddest loss and caused much resentment, especially since it had been founded by public subscription.

SUNNYSIDE

When you reach Cricket Hill Lane, cross over cautiously, follow the narrow path opposite through the gorse and then turn left on to a very bumpy road. Sunnyside was the name given to this row of houses which began to go up about 1850, though part of Magpie Cottage at the end on the right is thought to be mid-eighteenth century. The earliest were labourers' cottages - "two up and two down" - but have been enlarged to become comfortable houses in an agreeably rural position. Heather View, dated 1901, has a one-storey extension on the left which was Mr Bailey's grocer's shop in the 1930s. He also ran a Young Men's Class which consisted mainly of games, the young men being about twelve years old. ("Teenagers" had not yet emerged in the 1930s.)

Their sisters may have been attending Mrs Gulland's smocking class at her house, Little Croft, a short way down Handford Lane. She had started it a good many years before to amuse the little girls who lived on Cricket Hill, and while they learnt the skills of smocking she would read "good" books to them, such as "The Pilgrim's Progress" and "Heidi". It was a popular class and the girls produced excellent work that was shown at national exhibitions. When Mrs Gulland grew too old, new teachers and readers were found and the class was moved down to Yateley Industries where it continued until about 1980.

Further along, Chestnut Cottage, built in 1897 and now rendered white, represents innumerable neat Victorian brick cottages with slate roofs and a central porch. There was a little grocer's shop here too in the 1930s and '40s, whose owner, Miss Stevens, applied for a tobacco licence during the war, no doubt following a big demand from the servicemen stationed on her doorstep. In addition to such useful "corner" shops for Cricket Hill, older people remember tradesmen who called at the door: the delivery men from the shops down in the village; the cake-man on a bicycle from Fleet with fancy cakes in his side car; the knife-grinder; gypsies with clothes pegs and little packets of lavender; and the oil-man who sold soap and other household materials as well as paraffin for the lamps that were still being used in the 1930s. Electricity came to Yateley in 1933, but oil was cheaper, quite apart from the expense of installing electricity. Gas lighting was used as well but it cost more than oil so was often kept for special occasions.

You will see if you walk so far that the last house stands on the edge of a small wood, once the haunt of glow-worms. This has sprung up since the Second World War. A previous occupant who bought the cottage in the mid-twenties remembered there was then open countryside all around with no trees at all.

Return now along the bumpy road. The gardens behind these cottages slope down steeply to a small stream with a right of way alongside it. It has been little used in living memory and has probably now been incorporated into the very small gardens of the Tudor Drive estate on the other side of the stream. On that land beyond the stream, two narrow fields called Upper and Lower Hop Gardens are shown on the 1844 Tithe Map. Did they perhaps supply hops to the many ale-house keepers for their own brewing?

CASA DEI CESARI

Take the right hand fork of the bumpy road when you get back to the beginning of Sunnyside again. Common cow-wheat, a semi-parasitic annual with pairs of two-lipped yellow flowers, grows freely under the trees on both sides. Cross Handford Lane (with care) and go up the track on the opposite side. As you will see from the sign, the brick buildings on the left are the Casa dei Cesari, an Italian restaurant and hotel.

Rather surprisingly, a pair of 17th century cottages are embedded in the complex. They were a good deal enlarged in the early 20th century with a piece built on to each side and three steps in the front as was the fashion, and became a family home known as Cricket Hill House. For a time it served as an old people's home, and in the second world war it was used for storage by Reeves. After the war it was bought by Brigadier and Mrs Charles who opened a restaurant there in 1970[36], by which time their children were old enough to be cooks and waitresses.

Two Italians bought Charles's Restaurant in 1978 and gave it the splendid Roman name of Casa dei Cesari, meaning House of the Caesars. (Or, as the phrase book might put it: Kah-zah day-ee Chay-zah-ree, with the accent on the first syllable in each word.) The restaurant was enlarged and the hotel and conference rooms added a few years later.

The old coach house of Cricket Hill House is the long low white building end on to the path. Today it is a private house.

YATELEY BAPTIST CHURCH

You have now reached the Baptist Church. Its beginnings were in 1825 with the arrival from Reading Baptist Church of William Holland who started by preaching the gospel in the little cottage opposite - The Nest. He very soon felt he could venture to build a chapel on Cricket Hill and in spite of many obstacles Zoar Chapel was opened on this site in 1827, with William Holland minister[24]. The chapel cost £140[10].

Zoar Chapel

In accomplishing this so rapidly, he had the support of other Baptists in the locality and in particular of John Andrews Jones who was to become a well-known - and evidently somewhat fiery - Baptist preacher and writer. Jones had been ordained minister in 1816 at nearby Hartley Row (Hartley Wintney) where he remained two years before spending brief spells at chapels in various parts of England, becoming pastor of the Particular Baptist Church in Brentford in 1825[25]. It was Jones who from Brentford applied for the Dissenters' Meeting House certificate for the new Zoar Chapel at Cricket Hill in February 1827[30].

The congregation was soon augmented by a group of Strict Baptists from Blackwater who were unhappy with their new General Baptist minister. There seem to be few records of the chapel's early years, but the religious census of one Sunday in 1851 recorded 40 attending the morning service and 51 in the afternoon. (On the same day the parish church claimed about 300 for each service. The population was 833[28].) Nonconformist chapels, which had spread rapidly during most of the 18th century and the early 19th, were attractive to artisans, shopkeepers and labourers, who often saw the church as the domain of the gentry and the rich. The minister at the chapel, on the other hand, was like one of themselves[14].

Zoar Chapel was built of red brick with a slate roof in the classical style usual amongst nonconformist chapels at the time, having a simple pediment and windows set in tall arched recesses. It had seating for eighty, and a stove to heat it, but no means of heating the water for baptisms (by total immersion) which was brought in barrels from the pond on the common. Behind the chapel were stables, for quite a few families came in pony carts from some way off. All brought their lunch and spent Sunday there. A member who attended the chapel as a child in the early 20th century wrote of her enjoyment of Sundays which were set apart from the rest of the week, and how she felt part of a secure and close-knit community in the chapel[24].

The new church that replaced it opened in 1965. It is spacious and light and was designed to be very visibly a church from Cricket Hill

Lane, achieving this with the large east window and slender fibreglass spire. Set into the wall is the foundation stone of the first chapel, inscribed 1827[24]. The term Strict Baptist is no longer used; it is Graced Baptists who worship here today.

The walk has now ended back at The Cricketers and beside the sturdy batsman at his post outside, to remind us of the cricketing days of long ago. If you watch for long enough, they say, he will begin to raise his bat.

REFERENCES

1. Breckon, B. & Parker, J. *Tracing the history of houses.* Countryside Books 1991
2. Christison, M. Unpublished letters c.1970
3. Coleridge, G. In *The Times.* 18th April 1983
4. Dobson, E. *Rudimentary treatise on the manufacture of bricks and tiles.* 1850. Quoted by Tony Wright in *North East Hampshire Archaeological Society Newsletter.* August 1981
5. Garrett, B. *The Wyndham Family in Yateley.* In *Yateley: a parish through six centuries.* WEA Yateley Branch 1984
6. Hodson, Y. *Ordnance Surveyors' Drawings 1789-c.1840.* Research Publications Ltd. 1989
7. Holyroyd, E.M. *Tudor Yateley: families, livelihoods, and wealth.* In *Yateley: a parish through six centuries.* WEA Yateley Branch 1984
8. Horn, P. *The Victorian country child.* Alan Sutton Publishing Ltd 1985
9. Ives, G. *A walk in the past.* Unpublished. 1970
10. Lewis, D. *Yateley Parish Magazine.* October 1985
11. Marshall, S. *A History of Blackbushe Airport.* In preparation.
12. Mills, J. Diary 1876-80. Hampshire Record Office. Unpublished.
13. Nash, P. *Outline: an autobiography and other writings.* Faber 1949
14. Mingay, G.E. *Rural Life in Victorian England.* Alan Sutton Publishing Ltd 1990
15. Piggott, S. *Bronze Age and Late Celtic Burials from Yateley, Hants.* In *Berkshire, Buckinghamshire and Oxfordshire Archaeological Journal, Vol.32.* 1928
16. Renshaw, A. *Cricket on the Green.* Eversley Cricket Club. No date, 1987
17. Stilwell, G.H. (ed. S. Loader) *The History of Yateley.* No date, 1974
18. Stilwell, J.P. and E. *The Stilwell Family.* Unpublished c.1920
19. Stilwell, N. *Clooty.* Unpublished. c.1935
20. Stooks, C.D. *A History of Crondall and Yateley.* Warren & Son, Winchester 1905
21. Timms, M. *The future of Hampshire's heathland.* Hampshire County Council 1989
22. Vickers, J.A. (ed.) *The religious census of Hampshire, 1851.* Hampshire Record Office 1993
23. Ward, Y. *An Examination of Prehistoric Settlement and Activity in the Blackwater Valley and Floodplain.* Unpublished. c.1985
24. *150 Years of Growth for Yateley Baptist.* Yateley Baptist Church 1977

25. *Dictionary of National Biography.* Oxford University Press 1917
26. *Sheetlines. Journal of the Charles Close Society, No.34.* September 1992
27. *Commons Society Journal* 17 (4) February 1966
28. Enumerator's schedules for Censuses: 1841, 1851, 1861, 1871, 1881 and 1891. Hampshire Record Office
29. Hampshire Record Office: Q1/33
30. Hampshire Record Office: 21M65/F2/4/262
31. *White's Directory* 1859
32. Hilfield Estate Map 1810
33. *Ogilby's Britannia: The London to Lands End road.* 1675
34. Yateley Tithe Map 1844, copied by E.M. Holroyd
35. Yateley Vestry Minutes
36. Yateley Parish Council Minutes
37. Yateley Industries for the Disabled leaflet. c. 1975

I have also made use of the following:

Ordnance Survey Maps: 1816, 1871, 1896, 1912 and 1939.
Yateley: a parish through six centuries. WEA Yateley Branch 1984.
Unpublished notes by Sydney Loader.